PROFESSOR CLOWN ON PARADE

Rick Lupert

The poet's experiences in Burlington, Vermont, Waterbury, Vermont, Portland, Maine, and Hartford, Connecticut.

PROFESSOR CLOWN ON PARADE

Copyright © 2016 by Rick Lupert
All rights reserved

Rothco Press

Front Cover Design and Layout ~ Rob Cohen
Manuscript / Back Cover Design and Layout ~ Rick Lupert
Author Photo ~ Addie Lupert

"Breakfast at the Lang House" and "The Summit of Los Angeles Poets That Did Not Happen" originally appeared in *Poetic Diversity* Volume 11, # 2, November 2014 (www.poeticdiversity.org). "Everything in Vermont is Made in Vermont" and "Paddling to Canada" originally appeared in *The Bicycle Review* # 29, August 2014. (thepedestrianpress.weebly.com) "Here's the Problem" originally appeared in *American Mustard Second Volume*, January, 2015. "The Last Great Battle of Hartford" and "Oh Portland" originally appeared in *Yay!LA*, December, 2014. (www.yaylamag.com) "In Front of the Cryptozoology Museum" originally appeared in *Muddy River Poetry Review* Issue 13, Fall 2015 (www.muddyriverpoetryreview.com).

This book is protected under the copyright laws of the United States of America. Any reproduction or other unauthorized use of the material or artwork herein is prohibited without the express written permission of the author except in the case of brief quotations embodied in critical articles and reviews.

First Edition ~ December, 2016

ISBN-13: 978-1-945436-02-4

Published by Rothco Press.
www.rothcopress.com

Visit the author online at
www.PoetrySuperHighway.com

If the first beer doesn't taste like the second you've failed.

- Allen Pugsley

Often I think of the beautiful town that is seated By the sea.

- Henry Wadsworth Longfellow

If you combined a human and a cat, it would improve the human and diminished the cat.

- Samuel Clemens

Thank you Addie, Brendan, Elizabeth, E.J. Cohen, Daniel McGinn for being in Vermont at almost the same time we were, Alexis Rhone Fancher for your awesomeness in general (as well as the proofread and blurb), Harriet at the Old Round Church, Emilia at the M&M Bistro in Hartford, J.P. of the Hilton Hartford, Rodney Orpheus, all the people in Vermont who wanted to give us eco-friendly hugs, Ben & Jerry for inspiring us to go in an indulgent food tour of Waterbury, Vermont, all the people in Portland, Maine for putting your food in our mouths, all the people of Hartford Connecticut who stared at us in disbelief when we told them we were vacationing in their town, and the attractive staff of Rothco Press.

To Addie who lets me take her anywhere in the world as long she gets to decide where we eat.

ONCE AGAIN WE FLY TO THE EAST COAST

Derrick Brown says you should always start out with a short poem.

How's this one Derrick?

Here's the Problem

A third of the way to the airport
I realize I left my wedding ring at home.
As long as it's not a statement
        Addie says.

At breakfast in Terminal Three
my coffee mug comes with lipstick
from its previous user.

Addie tells me about how they
never clean glasses properly
in hotel rooms.

She doesn't want to go into detail
before our food comes
but the image is there.

The waitress tells us they've
run out of egg whites.
I wonder how that's possible if

they still have eggs.
Have they lost the technology which
allows them to be separated?

That is a question only assholes would ask.
It is too early in the trip to take that path.
so I keep it to myself.

Assholes I think...
And already this book is
unsuitable for children.

It is so presumptuous to
assume I'm writing a book.
I'm going to have to

earn my wedding ring back.
It begins by not putting my lips
on someone else's lipstick.

The coffee is okay.
The kitchen has figured out
how to provide egg whites.

My naked finger...
I've got twelve nights
to make this right.

Nightmare at Zero Feet

Outside the airplane window
I see a man carrying a red bag
adjusting his music player.

This is okay because
the airplane is still on the ground.
If we were already flying

and I saw that out the window
this would be a completely
different poem.

Bon Voyage

They tell us our plane
is continuing on to Paris
after it drops us off in Philadelphia.
At least they think they'll be
dropping us off in Philadelphia.
Now that we know this plane
is going to Paris, all bets are off.

Haiku

Wedding ring ads in
the airplane magazine mock
my naked finger.

And Now a Break for an Important Thought

I'm concerned the phrase
"In no time at all"
sets an impossible expectation.

Mooning America

For Brendan in West Virginia

Can you see my ass?
I'm in the right side of the plane.
I see a river.
Is that you?

Rocky Mountain Sensibility

While reading the in-flight news
I see an article about waitresses in Colorado
who are allowed to carry loaded guns.
Remind me when I'm dining out in Colorado
to order the *Whatever You Feel Like Bringing Me,
Ma'am* special.

WELL WE'RE LIVING HERE IN ALLENTOWN (FOR 2 NIGHTS)

New Potato

In Allentown, Pennsylvania
my father in law walks in from the back yard

a stack of fountain pens in his hand
asks my mother in law

Do you have an old potato you're not using?
She tells him she only has new potatoes.

He asks if he can just have part of one
and she explains, essentially it's all or nothing

when it comes to potatoes.
He wants to use the potato to clean his fountain pens.

She gives a new potato to the cause.
It's okay.

Getting more potatoes
is not really an issue.

Hierarchy

The car seat in our rental car
is so comfortable I tell Addie
I could nap while driving.
She shakes her head no
already laying down the laws
for this vacation.

Arthur Bucks up Against Independence

They named the hurricane Arthur
after my great uncle I presumed.
I begged him for a dollar once
while my mom was at work.
I wanted to buy her a present
from the garage sale next door.
He didn't want to give one to me
but I was relentless.
Later my mother told me
not to beg my uncle for money.
It's thirty five years later.
My uncle's body, long gone.
He hits the shore in North Carolina.
Fireworks postponed indefinitely.

The Slogan That Didn't Cover Everything

One sign off the highway says
Don't drive a lemon. It's good advice
but I wonder how they feel about bananas.

Forethought

One truck has had its right turn signal on for at least fifty miles. You've got to admire people who plan that far in advance.

Fourth of July

Our five year old
tells everyone at the party
that he chopped off my head.

I would respond but
I don't want to break character.

haiku

I saw a squirrel
in Lansing, Pennsylvania.
Gender uncertain.

Afterthought

Twenty miles later
the truck turns off its turn signal.
Anything's possible now.

Transfer to the 22 West

American flags at every *E-ZPass* booth
When I get back to Allentown
I'm going to pee like winter never ended

This Poem is Unnecessary

We pass by the hospital
where my wife was born.
I assume we don't need
to stop to see if she left
anything in the delivery room
since we are born
without possessions.
This is the kind of thing
no one else needs to clarify.

DRIVING TO BURLINGTON

It Just Does

The sign tells us we are
now entering New Jersey.
Addie asks how
that makes me feel.

Marketing

One sign says *Night paving begins in August.* Night paving. That's the hip version of road repair meant to appeal to the younger generation.

Another sign tells us

United States Equestrian Team
Next Exit

I wonder if they're all really there
ready to sign autographs and
offer free pony rides to the kids.

Driving New Jersey

We pass the Mahwa Wawa.
I won't mention it.

Turn

A sign on the highway tells us
Washington's headquarters next exit.

I hope they didn't put that up
until after the revolution

as the British might have seen it
and we would all be speaking English.

We

drive through
New Jersey
without stopping
as is our way.

I

wake Addie
to tell her
my head is full.

I Glance at Addie Longingly

I don't want to interrupt her but
I need her to type a new poem
She notices, knows what I want,
tells me to use my words please.
She's already typing this in so
I guess I didn't have to.

Nothing to be Done

One New Jersey license plate is just
the number printed on a letter sized piece of paper
flapping in the New York highway wind en route to Albany.
We should all chip in and buy Jersey some steel.
Anyway we just crossed into New York.
It's no longer my problem.

Public Service Announcement

In case you were wondering, yes
I did wear my red, white, and blue
American flag underwear yesterday
for the Fourth of July.
But it's not what you think.
I bought a new pair this year.
A more comfortable summer material.
So, update your *Rick Lupert Underwear Chart*, America
We'll compare notes on the internet later.

James Brown Gives Instructions on the Radio

There are New York State troopers
who I have no wish to meet.
So, I'm sorry, Mr. Brown,
we will be staying right *on our things*.
for the time being.

I'd like to call this one "The Perfect Storm" but that phrase is used twice in the poem so it's probably not a good idea.

Music from the film *The Perfect Storm*
comes on the radio just as we pass
New York's *The Storm King Art Center.*

Meanwhile, we notice the previous driver left
a stick of men's deodorant in the glove compartment
This is the perfect storm indeed.

Make Room on Your Bookshelves Oh Buyers of Poetry

The frequency of my observations while driving
is increasing at a frantic rate causing Addie to comment
This book is going to be two thousand pages long!

Perfect!

A sign tells us *Albany* with arrows
pointing in the direction we're heading
This is perfect because we're going to Albany
It would be frustrating if the same sign with the arrows
said *Not Albany.*

Reincorporation

Highway 87 is
some of the smoothest road
I've ever experienced.
Must be all the night paving.

Judgement

When we pass over Wallkill River
I give it a stern look and think *murderer*
thinking of my poor innocent walls at home
who would never hurt a fly and who often
let flies rest gently upon them.

I won't tell you what the town called Coxsackie makes me think of for the sake of the children.

Oh what the hell
It's testicles people!
If you live in Coxsackie you essentially
live in Testicleville.
That is all.

Common Sense

The sign somewhere in the middle
of the Adirondacks Mountains that warns motorists
of *low flying planes,* I think should instead be a sign
slightly higher that says *You are flying too low.*

Compassion Has Its Limits

I want to adopt a highway
but the cats are already too much work
and I think our son would get jealous.

Reincorporation Redux

There is no cell phone reception here in the Adirondacks. I'm going to throw my text messages off low flying planes into the Champlain Canal.

We Cross the State Line Into Vermont

I shake my whole body
pantomiming its adjustment into this new state.
Addie tells me it looks like I'm having a seizure in slow motion
Everything's a little slower in Vermont, honey I tell her
earning me my first real *look* of the vacation.

BURLINGTON

Hello Burlington

We arrive at Burlington City Hall
with plans to go on the *Ghosts Walking Tour*.
It's not a walking tour for ghosts, but rather
for people in which they point out where ghosts might be.
For all we know it's really for ghosts and they just have
people along to make sure the visible tour guide
doesn't look like a crazy person walking around town
talking to apparitions.

A professional skateboarder from Los Angeles
is filming a *move* off the City Hall steps.
He jumps over a *public safety* sign
rolls down a cement walkway and
into the center of the park.

The crowd gathered for the tour cheers him on
and after a self confessed *thousand tries* he makes it.
Everyone applauds. Burlington is known as the *friendliest city*
and we expect hugs to break out.

I keep this in mind as I deal with my own issues of personal space
as a guy sits down right next to me as we wait for our guide.

I get a text from a cousin in Plymouth, Massachusetts.
There is a gathering there. He tells me to buy a coat
And send him the bill. There's a factory here they say.

One that makes bears too
He doesn't like their taste though
unless they are vegetarians.

There were bear prints in the sidewalk
down Main Street.

I'll go anywhere
if bears are involved.

It Begins

A slow walking woman
dressed in all black
and carrying a lantern
approaches.

If this isn't our guide
I'm converting to
Satanism.

On the Cheese Trail in Vermont

Our first cheese in Vermont is at the Farmhouse Tap and Grill.
We wait a hundred years to be seated but all signs point

to this being a good idea. The walls are comfortable.
My head sinks in when I press against them.

I want these walls at home.
They also have a beer garden.

I want Vermont beer seeds to take home.
Maybe grow a bush. I could breed it with

a cow and have all the cheese I ever needed.
My short hair is out of control.

Soon the cheese will come.
I know exactly what to do with it.

From That Movie

A younger Paul Giamatti walks into the restaurant I want him to spit wine recklessly into a bucket and then drink everything out of the bucket. Instead they just take him to his table leaving me dreaming of Hollywood.

Addie tells me my beer is a pretty color.

I tell her she is a pretty color and I've only had
one sip so I know it's the me talking
and not the beer.

Every beer coaster has something different on it

and the one they give me says *He-brew*.
Later the waitress recommends the cheese
with *Moses* in the name.
I think we're being targeted.

Homonymania

Addie says Vermont is where Phish is from
but I hear *fish* and I'm trying to imagine how
they migrated from Lake Champlain to
the rest of the world.

Buttastic

The tables at Farm House Tap and Grill on Bank Street
are so close together, I'm getting a lot of waitress butt in my face.
Everyone is nice in Vermont Addie reminds me so I just revel in it.

Not Fooling

There's a *Festival of Fools* happening here in August. I tell Addie we need to come back then so I can declare myself their king. She doesn't disagree.

GOOD MORNING BURLINGTON

Breakfast at The Lang House

I
At breakfast
I put one of the napkin rings

(This is the kind of place that has napkin rings)
on my ring finger

just in case the server
of the other patrons

sees the regular ring on Addie's finger
and assumes scandal.

II
The couple next to us
discuss the drama of their lives.
They know a lot of liars.

I want them to go on
but a small dog has
run into the breakfast room.

They say his name is Willy
but our server is new so she
can't confirm.

I ask if I can
order a cat for tonight.
She's not sure the dogs

will allow it.
I'll talk to them
I tell her.

Anyway
the people who
know the liars

have left the building.
The dog their plan
all along.

We're Going to a Bear Factory Today

I'd like to watch them make a grizzly.
Maybe have a custom polar
to take home.
I'll name him Larry.

AT THE SHELBURNE MUSEUM

Paintings at the Shelburne

I
Louisine Havemeyer and her Daughter Electra
Mary Cassat 1895

Mother and daughter
look like they could be
brother and sister
or two girls recently married
thanks to Vermonter liberality.
Forget about the fact that
one of them is named *Electra*
That's an entirely different poem.

II
L'eglise de Vernon, Brouillard
Monet, 1894

This painting is bright
The church barely visible
Painted by Claude
before automatic exposure control
had been installed.

III
Les Glaçons
Monet, 1880

This one is Addie's favorite.
She wants to dip her toes in the cold Seine.
Perfect for early July Vermont.

IV
Petit gennevilliers
Monet, 1874

This one from a private collection
So I stare at it for a while
I may never see these sailboats again
Unlike Mary Cassat's
Mother Rose Nursing Her Child
Circa 1900
Which I'm pretty sure
I saw in the National Gallery last summer

One Less Thing

The bathroom here is unisex.
So I don't have to worry about
brandishing my genitals
as identification.

You're Welcome Government

We think one carriage in the Round Barn
is for the postal service, but it turns out it's a hearse.
I think I've just found the solution to
the U.S. Postal Service's money problems.

#mailorderdeadbodies

In the Circus Building

I
There are thirty four miniature elephants
in the Circus Artifacts Building
including two baby elephants
which are even more miniature
due to the nature of children and
how they are smaller than their parents.

P.S. There were three surprise
miniature elephants later in the exhibit
not included in the above count.

II
One miniature called *Professor Clown*
is near Russian Cossacks on parade.
Me and my ancestors get the two confused.

III
Addie wants to make sure I saw
the *monkeys on donkeys* miniature.
The fact they're being led by a clown
is the icing on our marriage.

IV
I may call this book
Professor Clown on Parade.
Look on the cover.
If that's the title you see
then we know that was
the final decision.

A Rail Car For the Presidents

features all the amenities
one could need to live
comfortably.

I could live on a train.

Then again I could
live in a box if
you poked air holes.

On The Ticonderoga

I
1955
Electra Webb nervous
about telling her cantankerous husband
she'd purchase the Ticonderoga.
A pause. He responds
Well Electra,
that's a hell of a lot better than
some of the other junk you've purchased
then continues his doodling.

II
Regarding the sounds one hears
when operating the Ticonderoga
Addie says she wants to hear the
difference between a *bell* and a *jingler*.
In fact, I think that's all she's ever wanted.

III
I salute a shuttle driving by from the bow.
A girl on board salutes back.
Addie is glad we had this moment and
I feel like the captain of the world.

P.S. I find out later
it was the aft of the ship
and not the bow.
A life time of naval academy movies
down the drain.

IV
I've located the *pressure water for ash ejector*.
That's one less thing to worry about.

V

A sign on the boat says
When bell rings go to your station.
I'm nervous I haven't been assigned a station yet.

Everything in Vermont is Made in Vermont

The hair dryers, the chairs, the art
There is no need for a Whole Foods here
because there are no partial foods here.
Even imported items are disassembled
and reassembled here with a hug and a smile.
Vermont is clean and whole.
Vermont is a bear cub.
Vermont is your recycled skeleton.
They'll use every part.
They'll grow your beard.
They'll condition the air with your breath.
They'll paper your napkin.
Vermont
made in Vermont
an American tradition.

At the Henry Tilton Straight Razor Collection

On average
a typical male
will shave
twenty thousand times
throughout his
adult life,
trimming twenty seven
feet of linear hair
from the more than
thirty thousand follicles
on his face
and neck.

I'd Like to See Photos

Dr. Jones Liniment is clarified as
Formerly Beaver Oil
leaving me awfully curious
as to how one harvests
beaver oil.

I'm Not Afraid to Make Up Words

I spend much of my time
at the Shelburne Museum
in the jail for my crimes
against Vermontity.

We Wander in and Out of More Shelburne Museum Buildings

I
The exhibit of *cocked hats*
makes me think I may never
have cocked my hats enough.

II
The exhibit of bed coverings
makes me realize we could save
a lot of money on art and decoration
by just hanging our bedspread on the wall.

III
I misread the sign that says *moisturizing foam*
as *moisturizing farm*, which explains my disappointment
when an assortment of wet sheep did not emerge when I
pressed the button.

IV
The display on the alarm in one building reads
Ready to arm.
Oh yeah alarm?
Well I am ready to leg.
Ha HA!

V
Addie's audible squeal of delight
when she encountered the sign that read

> *Stairs this way to dolls, dollhouses*
> *and automatons*

was worthy of archiving in the museum of
great sounds throughout history.

I hope the automatons do not develop
a collective consciousness and

take over western Vermont
while we are visiting.

VI
The expression on one doll
leads me to believe she was called
The Naked Doll of Unhappiness.

VII
One couple's lingering observations
of one particular doll house

      A) prevent me from looking at it
      B) prevent me from walking by it
      C) prevent me from living up to Vermont's
         expectations of happiness.
      D) all of the above.

VIII
The pride on the face of the
Sophisticated Monkey Drummer
is believable.

IX
Addie holds a pretzel over her eyes
and says "I found a mask!"
I don't know why we spent $18
to get into museums when all
we needed was a bag of snack foods.

At the Dutton House

I
When I ask for a pint of bitter
in the tavern in the Dutton House
to the imaginary person behind the counter
Addie chimes in
Make it a half pint for him.
I like it when she joins in
instead of walking away
when I do the things I do.

II
Addie is aware I've made it upstairs
in the Dutton House when she hears
my burp echo across the two hundred and
thirty four year old attic walls.

Home Improvement

One gallery room contains only two benches
faced at a single painting.
I suggest we clear out our son's room
and do something like this.
Addie is noncommittal to the idea.

Another Painting

The Death Struggle
Charles Deas, 1840-45

A man rides two horses
off a cliff holding a tree.
A Native American watching.
The man looks angry.
The horses afraid.
The only thing I want
to be in this painting
is the tree.

Haiku after the Room of Moose and Caribou Heads Followed by a Quote from Amélie Frank

I
How anyone could
kill these majestic creatures
Is far beyond me.

II
We are such a
wretched species.

I Don't Need Much

I find a little nook
between a stairway and a wall.
This is where I will be
from now on.

Addie asks What I Think is in the Electra Webb Memorial Building.

I tell her, like Vincent Price
the skeletal remains of Electra Webb.
Her blood and guts.

I'm not sure she hears this as she's
already making her way to the bench
shaped like two red lips in the middle of
a nearby field.

THE REST OF THE DAY IN VERMONT

At the Vermont Teddy Bear Factory

I
The first thing we see is a large silo
where they store the raw ingredients
to make bear.

II
Signs Inside the Bear Factory

Feel the inside of a bear
Bear Naked
Bear Bones
Embearassing
Bear Holes
Bear Food
Bear Mitzvah
The Bearst of All Worlds

III
Some of the bears are scented.
Root Bear for example.
I ask if any have authentic bear smell.
The guide laughs awkwardly.

IV
A sign in the gift shop says

> The majority of our bears are safe
> for children of all ages.

I'm particularly interested in
viewing the unsafe bears section.

Dangerous Proximity

On Shelburne Road
there's a *Pet Food Warehouse*
next to a *Subway*.

I wonder if anyone
ever gets confused and brings
their hedgehog a footlong.

Lupert Love Can Be Confusing

We walk out of the *Lang House Bed and Breakfast*
on the way to dinner and Addie says
it's gorgeous outside.
You're gorgeous outside I tell her.
Her eyebrow wiggling tells me
she's not sure if she should roll her eyes
or bat her eyelashes.

We Spot One in the Wild

We walk by a guy wearing a shirt that says
Party with Trees on it.
Fuck yeah party with trees
I tell him with the devil sign.

I've made a friend for life.

Eyebrow Technician

We pause on Main Street
so Addie can fix my eyebrows.
I never knew they could be broken.
But the amount of time she takes doing it
convinces me.

Ice cocktail

They serve Addie a drink with an ice log.
Now that's a cock-tail if I ever saw one.

Limits

There's an eatery here called
Single Pebble Restaurant.
Not sure what happens if
you want a second pebble.

Paddling to Canada

On the shores of Lake Champlain
a man in a kayak, just before sunset,
chases the sun.

After a while he takes a right
and, I assume, heads to Canada.
That's what's in that direction.

I never considered the kayak
as a form of international travel
before now.

I've never considered
a lot of things.

Advice for All Stores That Sell Just Socks

A sock store on Church Street has a sign that says Shoplifters will be prosecuted. I think the sign should say *Socklifters will be prosecuted*. Just so the shock of the crime is tempered with a little bit of humor.

Last Thought at 1am

I want to bottle this Vermont tap water. Then put it in the mouths of every Brita owning American. Let's be sweet with our liquids. Let's not understate the importance of hydration.

I Guess the Previous Poem Wasn't the Last Thought

The Lang House robes
hanging in our room
look like two extra people.
That's fine but we're not
paying the extra fifteen bucks
so they could have breakfast.

A DAY WITH THE GREEN MOUNTAIN BOYS

The Summit of Los Angeles Poets That Did Not Happen

For Daniel McGinn

In the morning
I receive a message from Daniel

from Los Angeles.
He is newly a master of poetry

and has left his wallet
at the Burlington airport.

He was heading home
diploma in hand

fresh supply of one dollar bills
left behind.

There will be no
summit of Los Angeles poets

in Vermont.
I will look for your wallet, Daniel.

Everywhere.

Today we are going to
the Ethan Allan Homestead

and a chocolate factory.
If I were your wallet,

that's where I would go.
Sorry we missed you.

Give Us This Day Our Holy Bread

The server at our bed and breakfast asks
if I want Jewish Rye with my breakfast.
I tell her no because I'm off duty but
after some thought I ask if they have Jewish Wheat
or even Episcopalian sour dough.
Not that I'd make that choice,
I just wanted to know if it was available.

Buzz

Autocorrect wants it to be *Bee and Breakfast* instead of *Bed* which would be a completely different experience.

Haiku

Bed and breakfast. The
serving staffw here are almost
as cute as Addie.

We Visit Ethan Allen's Homestead

It turns out no one knows what he looked like.
Although statues have been made and *so called likenesses*
have appeared on book covers and postcards.

Patriotic music automatically comes on when you
enter the museum grounds. Ethan Allen, Revolutionary war
hero. Ornery fellow with a heart of gold.

Promised he'd come back as a large white horse.
We put on the replicated hats of his time period.
Keep our eye out for a familiar mane.

Women Would Not Usually Catch on Fire

A common myth of the time
was that fire was one of the most frequent
causes of death.

Our guide tells us it's not true
as she showed us the fireplace and
explained about the garments they wore
which would smolder, but not burn.

Bare feet usually, to have a physical sense
of how close they were to the flames.
Women would not usually catch on fire
she told us which is a funny thing to say

and gives us a safer picture
of the time.

Museum Director Dan Wanders Off Into the Wilderness by the Winooski River

As the assistant director shows us the house
Museum director Dan walks out of the
administration building, heads behind us and
without a word wanders into the forest.
We assume we will find him later
nude by the Winooski River
as is his noon time ritual.

Sad Face Emoji

We find the one unfriendly Vermontian
in the form of the tour guide we didn't get
at the Ethan Allen Homestead.

Perhaps she was suspicious
finding us heading out of the grounds
unaccompanied by a guide.

She gnarls her lips like
she's about to spit chewing tobacco
on the ground in front of us.

We say *hello* and she
doesn't even avert her eyes.
Her tourist ducklings behind her.

She must be from Connecticut.
Still upset Ethan Allen didn't
take her with him.

New Religion

The tour guide at the chocolate factory urges
Let chocolate change your life.

Out of everything I've learned in Judaism,
school and on TV,

no advice has ever made more sense to me.
Yes, chocolate, I will go where you go.

Guide me to your bliss.

We Stop by the World's Tallest Filing Cabinet

It contains eleven cabinets with Roman numerals
up the side, probably indicating the year but

we're not sure as we don't speak the language.
You can't file anything anymore without getting

your feet wet through the weeds, wet with
Burlington's morning. Plus if you live in Los Angeles

or you're shorter than eleven filing cabinets
it's not so convenient.

Suspicious Chocolate Company Placement

The Lake Champlain Chocolate Company was built
right next door to Champlain Elementary School which seems
like judicious planning by the chocolate people
or, if the school came first, devious planning by a group of
fourth graders who infiltrated the city zoning commission.

At the Echo Aquarium and Science Center

I
The docent tells us to look into the bullfrog's eyes.
I want to tell him I never get past my wife's eyes.
But it is all in the interest of science. So I look
deeply into the bullfrog's eyes as she takes
an earth worm or three into her mouth.
I like eating too missus bullfrog.
Her eyes staring back into mine.
A deep connection formed.

II
There's not a lot to do here if you're an adult.
I think I spend more time at the hand dryer
in the bathroom than looking at exhibits.

The Human Alphabet

A gang of skateboarders
rides out of the Hilton parking lot.
One of them is the famous one from L.A.
we saw the other day.

They emerge like Adam West Batman
out of the Bat Cave. Except they give off
modern ruffian though just as much
a surprise.

The Hilton parking structure,
secret lair to the X Games generation. Or is it Y?
We're running out of letters to identify future
generations of disenfranchised youth.

I'm Sure Addie Doesn't Want This Included in This Book

Something's getting a little black
Addie says in the Himalayan restaurant
This could mean anything.

Haiku

Of all the swings on
the Burlington boardwalk, we
get the squeaky one.

Sunset Two On Lake Champlain

joggers and dogs of every size
boats
first sideways then
        pointing at us
couples
triples
families
soloists
Asians
Ice cream eaters
Asian ice cream eaters
women with shorts too short
        depending on who you ask
the sun keeps getting lower
the swing is squeaking
a homeless woman has made
        the next bench her home
a mother duck and her teenagers
the great state of New York
ferries bringing people and their cars
        from the great state of New York
an island
a mythical creature
and probably
        more fish than I can imagine
like a giant sturgeon
and a catfish whose whiskers
        remind me of home

I don't mean to judge

But t-shirts tucked into shorts.
I just can't.

At Vermont Pub and Brewery

I
Six beers come in six little glasses
This is what Greg Noonan did.
(Look him up.)

He died in 2009
at the age of fifty nine
his face too young.

Tulach Leis
the waitress tells us
was his baby.

Perfectly sour
Like a Flemish orchestra.
Well done Greg.

II
The painting of the cow
The Vermont Cow
is perfect.

Vermont is a prideful state

and not in an obnoxious way like Texas.
The girl who just came back from California
tells us she liked it, but after a week
she missed Vermont.

Every restaurant and factory boasts
the local products they use.
I've already mentioned the hugs and smiles.
Ice cream was practically invented here.

(or at least made famous.)
Ethan Allen may not have made furniture,
they may not know where he's buried.
But he forged a state

worthy of this pride.

WE PUT THINGS IN OUR MOUTHS IN VERMONT

Thoughts at Breakfast*

I wonder if Ben & Jerry's has a mascot.
Maybe a cow named Moobert.

I tell Addie when we get there
I'm going to march in and demand to see

Moobert. She doesn't react at all.
Is tending to her head, she tells me.

Later says she is just glad I didn't say
I was going to be nude

when I marched in.

*An uninspired poem title.

Green Mount Cemetery

I
The only mission of the parking attendant
at the athletic center next to Green Mount Cemetery
was to make sure I didn't park there.
He also hadn't heard of any cemetery near there.
I was going to have to *move my car on out of here.*
Find dead people outside of his purview.

II
For Britannia Bacon
1801-1888

At Green Mount Cemetery I learned
that Bacon died in 1888.

Imagine if we put every meat
in its own grave.

Or perhaps we do
and that's what plumbing is.

III
After visiting Ethan Allen's grave
where he may not be buried
we see smoke pouring out of
a lawn mower and I'm pretty sure
the men gathered around it had a
"Burn the remains"
look on their faces.

Haiku, Richmond Vermont

We're heading to the
Old Round Church. I hope they have
an old round bathroom

At the Old Round Church

Harriet
(who is ninety five)
in the Old Round Church
in Richmond, Vermont
(as opposed to Richmond somewhere else)
tells us we can do anything we want
in the Old Round Church
except for eat or destroy things.
You know how my mind wanders
(especially when I hear the word anything)
but I still managed to eat nothing
and destroy nothing
in there.

We Arrive at the New Holy Land

We follow the Winooski river
to Waterbury, Vermont,
home to everything Vermont has to eat
but, most importantly
Ben & Jerry's.

Everything here is tie died and covered in cows.
Every employee has a smile bigger than Vermont.
There's magic in the air and a free spin art station.
It's like visiting a real life Willy Wonka Factory.
Music from the sixties playing in the bathroom.

Oozing socially responsible.
Mandatory anti-GMO labels on everything.
You will make the world a better place
by putting this product in your mouth.
This is the Woodstock of ice cream.

No cryers allowed. Not possible here anyway.
These are the colors of happiness.
These are the cows of your delight.
Grab a pint and a spoon. This is happening.
The cow bell rings. We're going in.

Four Important Facts at the Ben & Jerry's Factory

I
Employees get to take three pints
of ice cream home every day.

II
Employees may not sell their free pints
but they can use them like currency in town
at willing establishments.

III
In the quality assurance room
they have something called
non-sterile pippets.

IV
The elevator up to
the *Cow Over the Moon Theater*
is called the *Vanillavator*.

Stop Two of Four on the Vermont Food Caligula Tour

Cabot cheese annex
Free cheese
I'll say it again
Free cheese and
Cheddar popcorn
And crackers with spreads
And maple syrup tastings.
I'm writing this on a cow bench.
I may never eat again.

(I'm going to eat again.)

I Eat Again and Again

You can sample cheese, syrup
ice cream, cider, donuts and
coffee in Waterbury, Vermont
unlike in Los Angeles where you
get what you get and you
don't get upset.

At the Cold Hollow Cider Mill

I
The website says they
*don't offer formal tours at
the Cold Hollow Cider Mill.*
I'm praying to *Jebus* that means they
offer all nude ones.

II
Addie is in a cheese coma.
So when I see another one of those things
where you can put your head through and take
a picture from the other side she tells me she's
done putting her head in things.

But I think that's just the cheese talking.

III
Graffiti above the hand dryer in the bathroom says

> *The star of Bethlehem.*
> *Be a rebel. Follow Jesus.*

No offense Jesus, but right now
I'm following the Vermont food trail
and am about to pray to a donut.

IV
Like the Native Americans
they use every part of the apple
at the Hollow Creek Cider Mill
honoring their *applecestors*
et cetera.

V
I wonder if the people who work here
are called *apployees*.

Caffeine Destiny

We complete our food tour of Waterbury, Vermont
at Green Mountain Coffee and Visitors Center
in the old restored train station. A woman greets us
when we walk in and talks to us for about fifteen minutes.
We don't think she works there but we feel very welcome.

On the Road Again

I'm driving through Middlesex, Vermont.
I'm kinda middle turned on.

I'm driving through Montpelier, Vermont.
There are masters degrees hanging
from the trees like fruit.

I'm driving through Twin Ponds, Vermont.
They must be fraternal because
one of them has the stink eye.

I am driving through Woodstock, Vermont.
It's like the one in New York only
a completely different place.

I'm driving through Killington, Vermont
and I mean it this time.

I'm driving out of Vermont into New Hampshire.
The *Welcome Center* is several miles into the state.
I guess they want you to really be sure.

We drive though a place called Contoocook, New Hampshire.
I have nothing meaningful to say about this.
I just want you know there's a town called that.

Foreshadowing Dinner in Portland, Maine

Central Provisions

One Yelp reviewer says
This place is fucking ridiculous.
Without reading the entire review I don't know if

it's the kind of place where, when you walk in,
they punch you in the face and spit on your genitals
or if the food's really good.

We read ahead and the reviewer says
Go there and get busy.
It is still unclear.

Addendum:
Having now eaten there
I can report it's the latter.

We meet E.J. in Concord, New Hampshire.

She tells us about the time she almost couldn't
get to the Halloween parties because she and her friends
dressed as Coneheads and the cones
attached to their heads, wouldn't fit in the car.

She tells us about when her mother was
getting ready to die. Wanted Sam, the family undertaker
to pick her up early. Somehow managed to
rearrange the furniture after she did finally go.
Her leg may still be moving.

E.J. buys us iced teas and french fries.
Reminds us of the many homes we have
all over the world. Inspires us to
get our own family undertaker.

There are a lot of Old White Bearded New Hampshirians Driving Around Concord.

I'm not sure what to make of it.

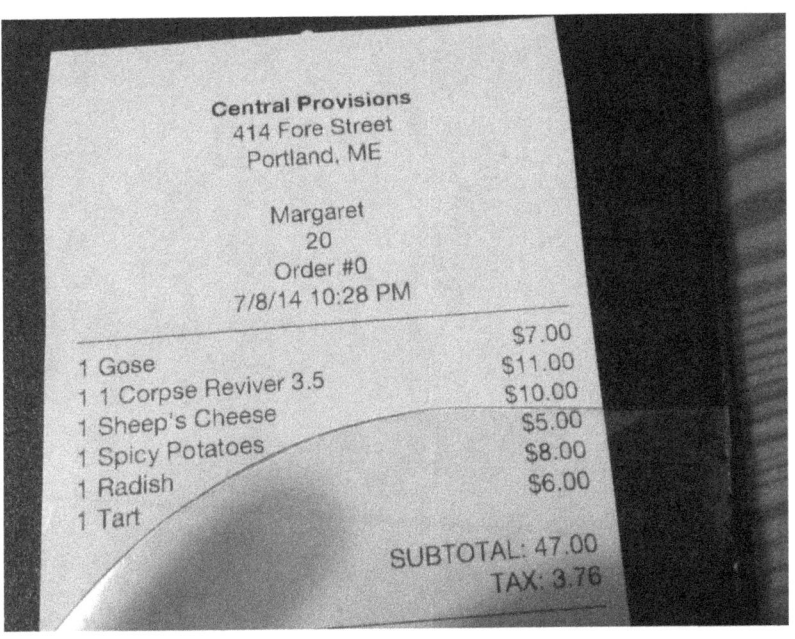

DRIVING TO PORTLAND, MAINE (NOT OREGON) AND THEN EATING THERE

There's a Difference

I see a sign on route to Portland that says

> *Old and Used Books.*

Since they differentiate I assume the old books were released a long time ago and never read which makes me sad for the authors.

Homogenization

We pass by a restaurant called *Payao's Thai Cookin'*
which is really the best of both worlds –
The world of people who like Thai food
and the world of people who like to say words
with a down home sensibility.

Driving Vermont and New Hampshire

Just passed by Nippo Lake.
Got me wondering
if there were any Nippopotamuses.
Dan Nichols says *there better be.*

We Pass by Hussy Hill Road

We've got to get to Portland, Maine for a late dinner. Otherwise I'd stop to check what that was all about.

We take a pitstop at the Kohl's in Rochester, New Hampshire to Use Their Bathrooms

I
A sign says *do not bring un-purchased items into the restrooms.*

What if I personally crafted the item
and brought it with me?

It looks like Kohl's needs to put up
a more detailed sign.

II
Kohl's has "iron free khakis"
which is great because the last thing
I want to worry about is metallurgy
when wearing pants.

Three Different Moose Signs

One sign warning Moose may cross the highway
is a picture of a moose.

Another is the word MOOSE.

A third is a picture of a moose with the words
"Moose May Cross."

There are so many ways to communicate
the potential movements of Moose.

I misread a Park and Ride sign as "Pork and Ride."

Just to be clear this was a misreading.
So you shouldn't go looking for a place
where you can park and get a good porking.

Truth or Auto Correct

One of these phrases is the correct one and one is the autocorrected one:

Caramelized Sheep Cheese.
Carmelite Sherpa Sneeze.

If you guess which is which you win a prize.

What we ordered at Central Provisions, Portland, Maine

1 Gose
1 Corpse Reviver
1 Seared Sheep's Cheese
1 Spicy Potatoes
1 Roasted Radishes
1 Tart

(The tart was the owner's mother's recipe.)

No Hurry

I tell Addie to take her time as she
finishes her drink. She says
oh yes, time will be taken
as she takes another sip.

Choice

*Would you like to
lick the cinnamon building*
I ask Addie.

No.
She would like
to smell it.

Portland's Ever Present Seagulls Make Themselves Known

We wake up to the sound of sea gulls
and our own sun beaming off the Atlantic Ocean

into our room. We couldn't find the blackout curtain
so it's probably 6:30 in the morning and we've got

vacation pillows on top of our heads blocking out
Portland's elements. The visual ones anyway.

You can't stop the seagull cries going into your ears.
I dare you to try.

Can you really trust a store called *Umbrella* that has nothing but decorative pillows with lobsters embroidered on them in the front window?

Your answer to
this question is
this poem.

At Hot Suppa

When I decide on the coffee
over the maple iced tea
the waitress tells me
We can just go from there.
It doesn't have to be the end.

Later when Addie asks about
the porridge versus *The Hollis*
she says *The Hollis* because
she's *feeling kind of eggy.*

I ask her
(the waitress in case this
has gotten confusing)
what it's like to feel *eggy.*
She says she's not sure.
Sometimes she *just says things.*
Leaves it up to us to interpret.

Oh yes *waitress* I get it.
Sometimes I just say things too
More then sometimes.

The eggs are coming.

TWO MUSEUMS

In Front of the Cryptozoology Museum

We arrive at the cryptozoology museum
ten minutes before they open at 11 am.

A woman gets out of her nearby car and tells us
the museum opens at 11 am.

This confirms what we read on the door and
what was mentioned earlier.

She just needs to count her money
she tells us, unlocking the door with

a plastic bag of bread pieces in hand.
We tell her we'll look for mythological creatures

on the streets until she opens. She says
Oh honey you'll find some.

The sounds of seagulls are ever present.
I want to tell them about the bread.

Sasquatch waits inside.

Inside the Cryptozoology Museum

I remember elementary school
In Dewitt, New York where my

friend Kevin told me, in third grade,
that the bathroom in our classroom

smelled like lemons which meant that
Bigfoot lived on the roof of our school.

I took it as fact and this was the
beginning of religion for me.

It's Real

A real live Australian armadillo lizard habitat
sits under a small Godzilla. They say you might not
be able to see the lizard because he hides in the
rock sculpture. There have been very few documented
sightings actually. A real live cryptic in Portland, Maine.

Maybe.

They Did This

People were painting in 1863.
People were seeing ships and islands
and hunters in trees.
People were putting them on canvas.
People were using colors,
autumns and summers.
People were putting their paintings in frames
and then in boxes.
People were housing their paintings in
frames and boxes larger then the paintings.
People were painting in 1863
I can prove it.

Named Art

I
Ulysses S. Grant Sculpture
Franklin B. Simmons, 1822-1885

Easily could have been called
Ulysses S. Grant With Sword
Sticking out of his Butt.

II
It's interesting that they call sculptures of heads *busts*.
You'd think they'd reserve that for sculptures of boobs.

III
Adrianna Hannaford
Charles Octavius Cole, after 1846

This could have been called
Baby with Old Lady Head
and Mismatched Shoes
Holding Weeds.

Moving on Up

We make plans to turn the nIneteenth century *McLellan House* into our personal residence. We're pretty sure we would turn the room labeled *private* into a massive private bathroom. But we're not sure about giving Jude the room across the hall since it has better views of the bay. We'd also have to tear down some of the modern buildings between here and there to improve the view. No use putting too much thought into it at this point.

haiku

Even inside the
museum, Portland's seagulls
are heard through the walls

She Knows

Addie wants to really emphasize to me
the sign on the gallery wall that says
Please keep a safe distance from the art.
She reads it to me slowly while
looking into my eyes.

Addie's Observations in the *Paintings of Maine* Exhibit

How could that one be untitled?
This one has too many eyes.
That one's kind if Dali-like.
This one was Bigfoot inspired.
I like it in here.

Tell Us More About the Paintings in The Museum

I
Two Boys in a Canoe
Neil Welliver 1966-69

A discussion about whether
the front boy is displaying
two buttons or his nipples
ends with a resounding
Nipples.

II
Jumping Boy
Robert Hamilton, 1989

Beware the spying hamburgers
jumping boy. There's no guarantee
the seals will protect you.

III
Three Female Cutthroats
Neil Welliver, 1968

Is three open mouthed fish
swimming to the left
(from our perspective)
Begs the questions
How does he know they're girls
and is he so sure of their intentions?

IV
Adventures of Huckleberry Fin
Asleep on the Raft (after Mark Twain)
Tim Rollins and K.O.S. (Kids of survival), 2011

Is painted on pages of Twain's book
which we'll try to remember when we
visit his house in Hartford, Connecticut
in a few days.

V
Icelandic Picnic
Louisa Matthiasdottir, 1968

Addie wants to borrow some eyes
from the painting in the other room
to put on the featureless faces
in this painting.

VI
Le salut
Paul Delvaux, 1938

A man tips his hat
to the woman in the square
with the exposed
naked butt.

VII
Hero and Leander
Robert Laurent, circa 1948

When your wife calls you over
and urges you to check out
"Pointy Boobs"
you know you've chosen the
right woman.

I'm not even going to mention
which painting had her favorite boobs.
It's becoming overwhelming.

GOOD MORNING PORTLAND

At the Portland Observatory

I can't tell you how afraid I was
I was going to accidentally throw my

phone off the Portland Observatory.
Stacy, our tour guide, who is a man

had only one request once we got to the top –
That we do not die.

His voice was like Garrison Keillor's
and I am the first person to tell him that.

I may just throw my phone off to ease the tension.
Not my whole body though.

The views would go away.
And so would I.

It Was a Big Boat

We see a boat for sale
so big it comes with its own
smaller boat.

Believable Lie for the Lazy

A gelato shop on Fore Street bills itself
as *Portland's only gelato shop*.
It is one block down the street from
another gelato shop.

Good Morning Portland

We walk past the *rock thinker* at the art museum.
The *Cumberland Club* has its doors closed.

The seagulls are out of control, or I might be
thinking of last night. *The Local Sprout Collective's*

doors are open. A couple discusses food equity.
I hear the words *kale* and *relationship empowerment,*

and *I went into the woods for a few days just to
think about things.* They start to compare crystals.

It's a granola business meeting I think.
On the east coast they call it *crunchy.*

It will take extra time to separate my eggs.
Our table marker is Stevie Nicks. She's

showing up everywhere these days.
Good morning Portland.

My feet on your ground today.
Your coffee in my mouth.

Call Joe

The largest building in town
flashes on an LED screen at the top
the time, the temperature and the words
Call Joe.

We think the mystery is solved at breakfast
when our coffee mug advertises *Joe Bornstein*
the lawyer who would like you to call him
and discuss your legal woes over a cup of
Joe.

As Mentioned Earlier

Our table marker
at local sprouts cafe is
topless Stevie nicks

(She might be bottomless too.
It's a sketch and hard to tell.)

What AM I Doing Now?

Addie gives me the
what's he doing now glance
and I try to think of what to do
to make the experience worthwhile.

Can you guess which word in this poem spell-check had an issue with?

The graffiti in the local sprouts cafe
says things like *You are enough*
and *Join the Activist Marching Band*
instead of the usual *fuck your ancestors*
and *For a good time call your momma*
I remember scrawled on the
shitters of my youth.

Oyward

As we get closer to
the Maine Jewish Museum
I'm praying to Jesus they have a
Maine Jewish Bathroom.

It's a thing
as we get closer to the museum
that my back starts to hurt.
Oy.

Jerusalem of the North

They say Portland was
The Jerusalem of the north

Every denomination meets here
Orthodox, Reform, to name a two.

There was a *fainting couch* on the third floor
for when the heat became too much for the ladies.

Restored to its original 1921 conditions.
Pews donated by a church.

An arm of the decorative crosses
on the hymnal holders cut off.

The Jerusalem of the north.
Beautiful.

Without all the division
of the one in the east.

Pass This On If You Know Him

I'd like Elton John to write
a Maine version of *Rocket Man*
he would call *Lobster Man*.

Either that or
Rocket Maine.
I'll let him decide.

1904

We look for signs of Judaism at
the old Shaarey Tphiloh synagogue.

Built in 1904 and now an office building
you can still see the synagogue's name

and the shapes of what must have been
glorious stained glass windows.

No sign of a mezuzah on the door and
when you walk inside, the sanctuary space

has been filled in with walls and several floors.
Instead of rabbis, it is lawyers and massage

therapists. We want to be archaeologists
and find a cubby that used to be the ark.

I think it's a real estate office now and we
don't have the kind of money it would take

to legitimately walk into that office.
There's no one to ask anything...

just a plaque on the wall telling us
what used to be.

The Tap Water in Vermont and Maine is Highly Drinkable

Unlike in Los Angeles where it is not
and you can't drink it anyway
because we're running out of it.

At Holy Donuts on Exchange Street

I
They serve the number one donut in Maine.
It has bacon in it so it won't be the
number one donut in our mouths.

II
The *Holy Donut* man says
There are no wrong choices.
We choose the Sea-Salt Chocolate.
It was not the wrong choice.
Seagulls outside sing
as we eat it.

III
I buy a bottle of water
from the donut man who tells me
you've got to hydrate your hustle.
That's exactly what I plan on doing.
I tell him.

Upon Seeing the Book "The Lobster Gangs of Maine" by James M. Acheson

The lobster gangs of Maine
weren't much of a threat
to the human population.

Occasionally someone got clawed
but that's about it.

Upon Seeing the Book "The Great Lobster War" by Ron Formisano

Sounds more ominous than it was.
A bunch of lobsters clawed each other

No rhyme or reason. Still
they don't like to talk about it.

When was the last time you heard
a lobster talk about anything?

Walking Tour of Old Portland

I
We spot a bottle of hot sauce in the docents back pocket.
I assume this is a prop for later in the tour but if it's not...

II
The hot sauce is
Captain Mowatt's Canceaux Sauce.
They say they've been *Burning Portland*
since 1715.

III
The tour guide is uncomfortable
telling us the purpose of the old brothel.
He tells us it was for *Happy Times*.
Everyone in the group just wants him to say
something a little naughty, add a little
edge to this experience.

He says *Portland ran out of lobster once*
and then said nothing else about that.

GOOD AFTERNOON PORTLAND

At Longfellow's House

I
The sounds of the fighter jets
that Longfellow never imagined
interrupt the *exterior of the house tour.*

II
The docent locks us inside the house
as she begins the tour.
Of course there's always her way out.

III
Anne Longfellow Pierce's permit
to build an outhouse was, reportedly,
the last one issued in the city.

IV
Things the docent said:

*If you haven't sat on a horse hair sofa
in the middle of winter in Missourah
you haven't lived.*

*There's a lock of family friend
George Washington's hair
around here somewhere.*

V
Henry's mother's bedroom.
Still no cat.

Ever since Da Vinci's house
in Amboise, France

whenever I enter a house
I always want there to be a cat

on the bed.

VI
Ann referred to
her three years of marriage
before her husband died as
her *little life.*

VII
Henry grew his luxurious beard
after his second wife caught fire
and he tried to save her
by wrapping her in a rug.
His face badly burned,
he never shaved again.
(And the manufacturers of rugs
never approached him with
any endorsement deals.)

VII
An untrue fact imagined after seeing
a hobby horse on the kitchen floor:

The wild hobby horse used to be
a delicacy in Portland as advocated
by the lobster gangs.

IX
This tour guide takes issue with
the Ethan Allen Homestead guide
and insists the second leading cause
of death amongst women
was burns from kitchen fires.

X
The Minuscule Luperts Enter The Kitchen

Generations of people
must have hit their head
on the coffee grinder mounted
on the wall by the back door.
Not us.

At the Shipyard Brewing Company

I
I have eight beers at the
Shipyard Brewing Company tour.

At least I think it was eight.
I have no idea how many beers

I had at the Shipyard Brewing
Company tour.

What?

II
We stumble out of
Shipyard Brewing Company
and, well I don't know.

III
I've got six beers in me,
maybe eight.

I'm wandering through Portland
looking for seagulls.

I want to take their pictures.
I want them to love me.

I see a Sign that says Simba Public Parking

You can only park here
if you are Simba the lion
from the movie.

If you are not Simba the lion
from the movie, you
should not park there.

Base Sensibility

Out of all the possible boat tours we could get on when Addie sees the one on which the passengers have coconuts with straws in them she says *that's the one*, having no idea the itinerary or cost. It makes sense to me as well.

haiku

The seagulls are the
ever present camera shy
soundtrack to Portland

GOODBYE PORTLAND

Raison D'être

I get the feeling
New Hampshire
exists just to keep
Maine and Vermont
from hitting each other.

Goodbye Portland

Oh Portland
I like you so much

but I'm not sure it's mutual.
On our last day

you serve me brown water
and call it coffee.

You paint my skin red with your sun.
You put a bug bite on my right pinky.

I've tried to photograph your seagulls for days.
You wouldn't let them standstill once.

But on the drive out if town,
just as we pulled out of the hotel

you have one of your biggest
take a shit all over our windshield.

There must be a weeks worth if seagull food
blocking our view to Connecticut.

Oh Portland
I have such a fondness for you.

But I'm not sure
how you feel about me.

Lies

A sign on the highway says
Watch for Moose in Roadway.
I watch for the longest time.
None ever come.

Unrelated Thought That Occurred to Me During the Trip

I know how fish communicate.
Ready for it?

Sea-mail.

I realize we're going to be in four states today

so I say out loud
We're going to be in four states today.

Addie responds,
Ah, New England.

Kind of like when Harrison Ford
popped up out of the Venice sewer

in Indiana Jones and the Last Crusade.
Please read this poem again and

have the Indiana Jones theme fade up
towards the end of that last line

for maximum effect.

I Can't Prove This

E-ZPass is for lonely people.

VACATION IN HARTFORD CONNECTICUT

We eat maple popcorn from Vermont on the way to Mark Twain's house in Connecticut.

It's what he would've wanted.

At Mark Twain's House

Mark Twain lived on Asylum Street.
It's how he got his hair.

Technically he lived on *Farmington*
but the street on the other side of the house

is *Asylum*. It's also possible
that Asylum Street wasn't there when he was

in which case this poem
is a poorly fact-checked lie.

A Few Assorted Mark Twain Facts and Quotes Because I'm in a Mood

I
Mark Twain wrote
report cards to
the phone company.

II
I have sampled this life.

III
All I do, know or feel, is,
that I am wild with impatience
to move-move-MOVE!
I wish I never had to stop
anywhere a month.

IV
At the age of seventy-one,
Mark Twain started wearing
an all white suit in public
which he called his
dontcareadamnsuit.

V
I believe our Heavenly Father invented man
because he was disappointed in the monkey.

Vacation in Hartford?

The confused look on anyone's face
When we tell them were vacationing in Hartford.

I've never heard of anyone vacationing in Hartford
they all say.

*You've got one of the oldest museums
and the Mark Twain house*

and a Lilly pond, I say, defending
their own town, to them.

You're vacationing here?
the waitress asks us

and then quickly points out the synagogue
across the street, built in 1872.

She becomes our tour guide.
We almost forget to order food and

ask for the check when she tells us
It hasn't been a synagogue

for twenty years.
Dave Matthews is playing

somewhere in town costumed players
from the convention litter the streets.

We eat dinner across the street
from a synagogue built in 1872

It's 2014 and the building is for sale
Call *Chozick Realty* if you're interested.

At City Steam Brewery

The singer is good.
All covers. He handles it.
But he clears the room
because people just want to talk.
Even we leave, and we love
when people make music
out of nothing.

We Arrive at the Hartford Chinatown

It's too small to see
You only get one store
with a sign on it that says
Chinatown. Still were
happy to have found if.

Sadly it's for rent.

The Minimalist Aesthetic

GOOD MORNING HARTFORD

Breakfast

We have the most dynamic person
in Connecticut as our waitress.
She sinks her head in shame
when she informs us they
no longer serve the quiche of the day.
The *butternut squash omelet*
looks promising though and
there are fresh blueberries
at the buffet so we may be alright.

The place is called *M&M Bistro*
and we're trying to figure out
how to pronounce it
or what it stands for.
Mmmmm or
Mandm or
Man and Moman

Addie heads off to the buffet.
In the mean time the omelets
have arrived

I have to go now.

The Hotel Manager

when dealing with our cheese-less omelet crisis
is bewildered to discover we are vacationing in Hartford.

He says he has a hard time considering Connecticut
to be a part of New England.

We spend a lot of time convincing
the residents of the greatness of their city.

The Mark Twain house.
The oldest art museum in the United States.

We're not sure we're believers either but
the missing cheese earns us free parking

and cocktails.
Or maybe he just feels bad we're in Hartford

calling it a vacation.
The whole day is ahead of us.

We're going to take it
one minute at a time.

At the Wadsworth Atheneum

I
The biggest question of the day
is whether to start or end with
the European impressionists.

Should they be the set induction
providing context for the rest of the day?
Or a reward for the hard work of
looking at art?

We arrive on *Family Day*
second Saturdays,
free for all!

Still, we announce to the
ticket ladies upon arrival
we are a family.

It works.
We don't even have to show
identification.

This is the
oldest art museum
in the country!

We take our free paper tickets
and go to look
at something.

II
The Battle of Orlando and Rodomonte
Battista Dossi, 1527-30

One of them is naked.
The other in full armor.
As if Rodomonte's job
was to keep naked people
out of the castle.
He glances nervously back.
Naked Orlando is
getting too close.

III
A woman is explaining a painting
to Addie in the next room.
I avoid the encounter.
The last thing I need this morning
is strangers explaining things to me.
I had enough of that at breakfast.

IV
Claude Monet Painting in his Garden at Argenteuil
Renoir, 1873

This one sends me into a multilayered
moebius strip of craziness.
I want to see the painting of Renoir
painting Monet
painting his garden
painted by Monet.

V
Standing in front of Monet's
The Church at Vernon, 1883
Addie queries
How does he do that?
I'd love to see Monet paint.
I begin working in the technology
to make this possible

VI
Bathers
Eugène Delacroix, 1854

I love the concept of *Bathers:*
Let's get some naked people in
a stream. Don't forget the swans.

VII
Great American Nude #69
Tom Wesselmann, 1965

One nipple points to the sky
like the Fourth of July.
I'm not sure how 'great'
she can be though
with half her head missing.

VIII
White #15
Glenn Ligon, 1994

This painting called *White #15*
is all black. I hear it took to #37
before he got it to be white.

IX
Addie heads into the next gallery.
I head into the bathroom.
Ahh to be young again.

X
Bluewald
Cady Noland, 1989-90

Bluewald's got an
American flag handkerchief
coming out of his nose
His very breath is liberty.

XI
Apparition of a Face and Fruit Dish on a Beach
Salvador Dali, 1938

Dali's *Apparition of a Face
and Fruit Dish on a Beach*
reminds me of my time
spent as an apparition of a face
in a fruit dish on a beach.
Ahh to be young again.

XII
The Five Strangers
Yves Tanguy, 1944

Tanguy's *The Five Strangers*
is well named.
I don't recognize any of them.

But you know what they say:
A stranger is just a surreal
multi-colored shape you
haven't met yet.

XIII
Autumn in the Village
Marc Chagall, 1939-45

depicts a fiddler in a tree with a goat.
This was painted after zoning laws
came into effect prohibiting fiddling
on roofs. The goat is just for comfort.

Below a topless woman lays on a roof.
It will never be illegal to be a topless
woman on a roof.

XIV
Whenever I see old guns
I want to check with you
to see if you have any messages,
any further correspondence.
I want to keep your dialogue open.
Make sure they know it wasn't
just for the project.
That's the kind of thing
that can delegitimize
an entire experience.

XV
They're cleaning up the art
from the waves project
now that it's past one o'clock
and the activity is
officially over.
As they drag the
connected pieces
out of the gallery
it does sound like waves.
I guess the tide's going out
I tell to anyone who
might want to listen.

XVI
They bag up the
Paper waves and
Take them out
Like the tide.

XVII
The Lawrence Tree
Georgia O'Keefe, 1929

They should call this one
The Octopus Roots Tree.

XVIII
Beauty Contest: To the Memory of P.T. Barnum
Florine Stettheimer, 1924

I hope they hold
beauty contests
to remember me.

XIX
Homage to the Square: Yellow Echo
Josef Albers, 1957

It's nice to see the square getting some props.
Shapes so often get used instead of honored.
Not sure why it has to share the stage with Yellow.
Maybe Yellow brought in bigger donors.

XX
The Young Lady with the Shiner
Norman Rockwell, 1953

You should've seen the other guy.

Someone's punched her in the eye
The principal and the teacher don't seem
happy through the office door.
She's sitting on a bench outside.
Bandage on her knee.
Couldn't be happier.

XXI
Still Life with Watermelon
James Peale, 1824
A Slice of Watermelon
Sarah Miriam Peale, 1825

A family of artists
painting watermelon
Father
Daughter
Still life
Then slice
They hadn't invented
seedless yet.

XXII
The painting Peale family
named one of their children
Rembrandt. He had no choice
but to go into the family business.

XXIII
Many paintings of Niagara Falls
North America's greatest *wonder*.
I stood on that shore, a hundred
and fifty years later not imagining
paintings hanging in Connecticut.

XXIV
If you want to be
proud to be an American
go to the Wadsworth Atheneum.
Look at the paintings of America
painted by Americans.
The grandeur.

XXV
Gremlin in the Studio
Martin Johnson Heade, 1865-75

Surrealism began in 1865
when a gremlin
lifted up the bottom
of the landscape portrait
to allow water to leak
out of the painting
onto the studio floor.

XXVI
Husband and Wife
Milton Avery, 1945

He is Mister Orange Face.
Her maiden name was *Miss Green Face.*
They have a dog. (not pictured)

XXVII
It says *No Refunds* on the zero-dollar
Free Saturday Wadsworth Atheneum tickets.
Somehow I still manage to get them
to give me all my money back.

Eating Cheese at the Museum Cafe

Eating a plate of cheese
will never go out of style
with the Luperts.

We are experts in
turning plates of cheese
into empty plates.

Addie's secret mission
is to eat the rest of the cheese
using the pretzels she
had stored in her purse
without any of the staff
noticing the contraband.

I swallow a grape seed
and as the tale goes
a plant sprouted in me.
So, if you need grapes
I've got them for free,
year-round. I want Addie
to swallow a seed so
we can start an orchard.

At Bushnell Park

I
A pigeon vies for my attention
like it thinks it's a seagull
or something.

II
The Lily Pond at Bushnell Park
has no lilies in it, and, in fact
one resident was surprised
to find out it was called
The Lily Pond.

III
We watch the Bushnell Park Carousel
make its rounds, like any grand old carousel.
Thirty six jumper horses, twelve stander,
two chariots and a Wurlitzer 153 band organ
with its standard, slightly off-key music
happening in this spot since 1914.
The painted ponies go up and down.
Only a dollar a ride. You can give more
to help feed the horses. We recommend
you do.

IV
Soldiers and Sailors Memorial Arch
is closed for renovations. Sigh
Another thing we can't go up
on this trip. First, Portland's *Head Light,*
and now this. At least there was
The Marine Signal Tower.
It's not a legitimate travel experience
unless we've gone up something.

V
It is Saturday night.
They're keeping the carousel open
long after the scheduled five o'clock closing.
As long as there are people who still want to ride
the Sabbath extends beyond its natural boundaries.

VI
We hear the last crank of the carousel organ.
They're closing the doors. We may never
see these horses again. I tell one of them
I know your sister in Griffith Park.
She maintains her look. A standstill
gallop. Worth so much more
than a dollar.

VII
I spot a stone structure with a hole in it.
Let's go take a picture in that hole
I shout to Addie.
I've always been a sucker
for a good hole.

VIII
The Charter Oak went down years ago.
Now there's a building where it stood
and a plaque nearby. I like to stand where
stuff was, but I'm not sure I can abide this.
As if a building could stand for a tree.

IX
There are no instructions
as to what to do at the
Pump House in the park.
I'm imagining all the kinds
of pumping possible
hoping for a match.

X
We stop by the Bushnell Pump Station
to get in some early evening pumping.
They are closed. We will have to
do our pumping elsewhere.

Sorella

I
Addie finds it's unsanitary for me
to put the pizza tray stand on my head
and nothing I can say can convince
her otherwise.

II
I'm not really sure how something
can be *extra virgin*. I mean it seems
like an all or nothing kind of thing.

III
We are seated by the pizza oven.
Not close enough for the heat to bother us.

Just enough so we can enjoy the show.
The dough tossing. The long slips.

The perpetual fire. Thick slices of
buffalo mozzarella, and a sea of

red sauce. In the brick oven
For only two minutes.

How's that possible
Addie wants to know.

I don't know but my pizza canoe
is ready to sail this pie home.

IV
Addie says
if we had the dough from Portland
and the sauce from here in Hartford
that would be *shoot me in the head pizza.*
There is a pause and she clarifies
shoot me in the head good.
I understood what she meant.

Everything is Free in Hartford!

Free breakfast earns us
free parking, somehow.

A free cocktail is on the way
because of missing cheese

on the free morning omelet.
Free Saturday at the Atheneum.

Oldest Art museum in the country!
We walked right in there. No charge!

Free tour at the Old State House
with free views of a two headed cow.

Free three dollars off our pizza at the restaurant.
For no reason at all!

Heading to the free Riverfest
with free bands and free fireworks.

Did I mention the free cocktail
which is coming later?

We're leaving Hartford
with our bellies full

and more money
than we came in with.

You on a budget?
Thinking travel?

Let me tell you.
Hartford Has it.

Not looking forward
to the real world

The rest
outside of this magical

bubble of financial liberty.
Buying my food.

Paying to get in places.
Hartford, you are the place!

I'm going to call my
financial institutions and

tell them I'm moving on.
I'm going to throw my wallet

in your river tonight.
Watch it sink to the bottom.

Not think of it
again.

It's About to Happen People!

A giant robot stands on top of the Hartford Science Center ready to walk off the roof and destroy downtown.

And why shouldn't it?

Riverfest

All of Hartford has gathered
for the running of the fireworks

along the Connecticut River.
East Hartford, regular Hartford

they are all here.
The bands are playing

It is only so often
their sky explodes.

Dialogue While Sitting on the River Bank Waiting for the Sky to Explode

Addie:
If there was a guy
walking by right now
selling Rita's Water Ice
I'd buy some.

Rick:
If there was a guy
walking by right now
collecting urine
I'd give him some.

Addie:
If there was a guy
walking by right now
selling chairs
I'd buy some.

Nightbaude

The Connecticut River goes all the way
up to Quebec, Canada. It's responsible
for the boom of this town and the one
in the sky tonight. We've been to Canada.
We've been here. We are here now.

The explosions wake the full moon
who creeps up over East Hartford's trees
to see the ruckus. She is full tonight
like my love for America, and for you.

Yes, my love, the earth revolves around the sun.
The moon revolves around this river.
and any place you might be, heavenly body,
Quebec, Canada or Hartford, Connecticut.
I will always revolve around you.

ConnectiCon is at our Hotel

Two days in and I'm
finally ready to get on board.
I put on my *Doctor Who* t-shirt
and walk into the hotel cafe
proudly ready to state
Hello nerds I am your king!
The convention is over today
so they're all kind of over it.
All the cosplayers of the last
couple nights look just like
people...and my dreams
of becoming the nerd king
fade away with a slow shake
of Addie's head.

Addie Has a Whole Plan for Breakfast

She's been thinking about it since back
in the room when I was still only
dreaming of being awake.
She's even found a way to
compensate for the giant forks.
She's giving me the details
but has to pause when she
points out the fruit she's
assembled from the buffet.
All the pretty colors.
I love fruit she says
trying not to cry.

The Last Great Battle of Hartford was Fought in the Elevator at the Hilton

for J.P.

It started last night
when the crowd from the multi-genre Sci-fi, fantasy, et cetera
ConnectiCon conference ended their evening activities
at the same time that the Dave Matthews Band concert
attendees ended theirs.

Both groups descending on the Hilton
from different directions on Trumball Street,
not to mention the locals who were filing away from the river
all charged up and patriotic after viewing the annual
twelfth of July fireworks

The police did not know what to do
as they watched the disparate groups converge.
On one hand, the ConnectiCon folks were all armed
with toy weapons and no pants.

On the other, the Dave Matthews disciples
appeared fiercely mellow and had all probably
done a lot more drugs that evening.

As it turned out the only casualty was the bartender
who kept confusing the specialty cocktails made
for the two different groups.
Man, you do not want to serve a "+2 Dragon Ball Fire Ale"
to a Dave Matthews fan. Conversely if you give one of the

Con kids a "Let's Just Take it Easy" he'll hit you with the saddest look you've ever known.

In the elevator on the way to check out,
one woman wearing a Dave Matthews t-shirt
avoided eye contact with the man who raised his arms
to cover the Cyberman on his.

Both got off the elevator unscathed
The locals from last night had no interest in taking sides
once they saw the girl with the pink hair, and the tail.
They just went home.

The Most Dynamic Person in Connecticut

Emilia is our waitress again today.
It doesn't stop the kitchen from
getting my order wrong again.
Yolks instead of whites.
The hash-browns not as done
as God intended.

ON THE WAY TO AND INSIDE THE NORMAN ROCKWELL MUSEUM

John Crapper Leaves Town

I see the army of portable bathrooms
from last night's *Riverfest* heading north
on the highway away from Hartford
and into Massachusetts where
Connecticut often disposes
of such things.

Each one like a little soldier
ready to dump its payload on
appropriate military targets.

Look out Massachusetts
fireworks are coming.

The Sign that James Brown Wrote

A sign on the highway says
Breakdown Lane Ends 1000 Feet.
Addie and I quickly each take a solo
thinking this might be our last chance.

Three Days Later

Addie cleans the seagull poop
off the windshield at the
Blandford Service Plaza
in Massachusetts
nostalgically.

Road Poem

I
The license plate of the Audi in front of us says "fly".
I wonder if the license plate on his plane says "drive"
or the one on his ass says "anything but this."

II
Another car has
a bumper sticker which reads
I love my gopher.
That's great lady but
you're not gonna love it so much
when it eats down your house
for the source materials to build
a dam in your bathroom
for when its cousin, the beaver
comes to visit.

(The truth is in the middle of writing this poem I realized it was beavers
not gophers that built dams; so I had to pretend the two were cousins to
make it work. I could have written something about the holes the gopher
would have dug under the house, but I didn't find it as compelling an
image. I hope you don't think I pulled a fast one and are willing to go on
to the next page. We're getting close to the Norman Rockwell Museum
and I think it's going to be pretty good.)

American Town

The bucolic setting of the
Pleasantview Motel just outside
Stockbridge, Massachusetts
surrounded by forests and
the cleanest air you've ever breathed.
There's a farmers market just up the road.
If TV and movies have taught me anything
it's that many murders happened in this hotel.
Their bodies dragged off into the woods
to serve the purposes of evil.
Welcome to Stockbridge my friends!

Not a Haiku

Oh the mighty constitutional
at the Norman Rockwell museum
America, America, America!

Also Not a Haiku

A sign on the door
inside the men's bathroom says
please open door carefully.

The last time someone
opened this door, Connecticut
fell into its river.

It's a wonder my paintings don't explode

said Rockwell describing his
"terrible" painting methods.

All of America is glad they don't.
But imagine the stories of

the first and only viewings that
could have been if they did.

Saturday Evening Post

Rockwell's photo like sketches could be matched by no camera other than the human eye.

He had a knack for seeing how high eyebrows could go.

December 4, 1920

Santa graced the cover of
The Saturday Evening Post many times
In 1920 he looks at an expense book
while hovering over the
Naughty and Nice book
like many parents today.

June 14, 1924

A pirate
years before Johnny Depp
graced our screens

August 30, 1924

A boy tries to woo a girl
with an accordion.
The look on her face,
she thinks he's cute
but an accordion is
never the way to go.

April 24, 1926

Maybe the same couple
their backs turned to us.
They have a dog now.
The accordion is gone.

Sept 22, 1928

They're older now.
He's got an ukulele.
The look on her face,
maybe it's not the instrument
but his skill on it.

She's still with him.

May 9, 1934

They're arguing over an urn
Maybe grandpa is inside.
A hookah on the floor.

Dec 21, 1935

Santa somehow looks
much older.
The Post is still
only five cents.

April 11, 1942

The Post doubles in price.
The war is here.

April 3, 1943

They're an old couple now.
He looks longingly into her eyes
over a checkerboard.

November 24, 1945

Their son, the soldier,
returns home.

They're going to make
a pumpkin pie.

August 30, 1947

Their grandchildren come to visit.
The lead *Post* article wants to know
Should husbands be babysitters?

December 27, 1947

The year is almost over.
The woman is so tired.
The Post is now fifteen cents.

August 20, 1955

A man carries off a mermaid
in a wooden cage. She seems
pretty happy about it.

December 29, 1956

A young boy discovers
his father was Santa the whole time.
A red suit in the bottom drawer.

October 21, 1959

The family tree.
Everyone is included.

We were born from pirates
and eventually became children.

September 16, 1961

The artist draws a
younger version
of himself, or

the artist draws
another artist. The Post
is now twenty cents.

This issue went to
WC Luzier in
Morgantown, West Virginia.

December 14, 1963

Rockwell's last cover
after forty seven years
Kennedy says goodbye.

I Know Everyone in Stockbridge

Rockwell spent the last twenty-five years of his life in Stockbridge, Massachusetts.

The best America had to offer, he said.
I know everyone in Stockbridge, he said.

Unlike in Los Angeles where I don't even know half the people by sight or name.

Documentary

The Rockwell film
is narrated by his son Peter
like a third person narrative pretending
they weren't related.

Represent

He painted a lot of Santa
but not one of Hanukkah Harry.
I thought it might be because of
a *Saturday Evening Post* policy.
Like the one that caused him to
paint out an African American
because he wasn't depicted
doing a service job. But
it turns out it's because
Hanukkah Harry wasn't invented
until the nineties, when Jon Lovitz
brought him to life on our
Saturday evening teevees.

Also, At the Rockwell Museum

I
Kellogg's Cereal Box Covers
Norman Rockwell, 1954-55

I like Tony the Tiger.
But to live back in this era
with these kids
on my cereal boxes
would be divine.

II
Market Day Special
Sun-Maid Raisins advertisement
Norman Rockwell, 1926

Oh Norman,
you make me want to eat raisins
eighty seven years too late.

III
Ballantine and Sons Beer and Ale Advertisement
Norman Rockwell, 1941

This old guy wants me
to have a sandwich
and a glass of beer
He's got a fountain pen
in his ear.
Who am I to say no?
Money well spent
Ballantine and Sons.

IV
Sketch of Cats
Josephine Verstille Nivison Hopper

This sketch of six cats
big blank space
probably meant for me.
The artist and I just
hadn't met yet.

V
Checkers
Edward Hopper, 1928

Never
play checkers
with a clown.

VI
The Engagement
Edward Hopper, 1921

Angry Colonel Sanders,
not so sure about bringing
uppity crew cut boy
into the chicken empire.

VII
Mothers Day Card
Edward Hopper, 1927

Different Interpretations:
I say *Hi mom,* you're a cow.
Addie points out the young calf suckling
at the mother's teat.

The Rockwell Museum

in the middle of sort-of-nowhere
Stockbridge, Massachusetts
is more crowded than any
of the big city museums
we've been in this week.

(In case you were wondering about
how wide his appeal was.)

Green

We're not as excited about the exhibit of
Edward Hopper's work at the Rockwell museum.
But the deep aqua green color they chose
for the middle gallery's wall is awesome!

Half and Half Juice Drink

At the museum cafe
Addie stumbles over the
drink I'm having, calling it
half an ass pop.

She is right to point out
printing the word RELAX!
in all caps followed by
an exclamation mark
inside the the bottle cap cover
may not do the intended job.

Ringing Rockwell's Bell

Outside of the museum
a sign says

Ring the bell if
you enjoyed your visit.

I ring it once.
Addie rings it twice.

We both enjoyed our visit
the same amount.

She's just
a wild woman.

In the Car

A Rockwell bug
flies into my eye.
I don't see it fly out
I guess it's coming
back to LA with me.

VACATION
DENOUEMENT

Our Last Drive

Back to Allentown,
the sun hides away
like it did last year
when we drove from Baltimore.
It knows the vacation is done.
Figures we won't need it today.
Hides behind a cloud.
Waits until next summer
to greet us again.

We Pass by the Town of Climax, New York

Sorry *Climax*. I shot my wad
back in Stockbridge, Massachusetts.
Metaphorically speaking of course.

haiku

Rain washes away
the last remnants of seagull.
We were never there.

Entertainment

Addie looks a little bored in the car, so
I do a little puppet show with my left hand.
Unfortunately, without the use of my right
which is busy steering the car, the left has
no-one to interact with, and the performance
lacks soul.

Addie seemed to enjoy it, however.
So that takes care of that ten seconds
of this three and a half hour drive.

Notes for Future Destination

We pass by *Wee Wa Lake*
which is right next to Tuxedo Lake.
The consensus is we'd have more fun
at Wee Wa Lake.

Night Pavers to the Rescue (Ideally)

New Jersey has some of the
bumpiest highways we've experienced
in five states.

They should import some of the
famous New York night pavers
to smooth things over.

At the Philadelphia Airport

I stood next to the sign that said
Please Touch Museum for hours

Nothing happened.

Sexual Innuendo in the Philadelphia Airport

I wonder what goes on in the "minute" suites.
I feel I'd need more time.

Sexual Innuendo on the Airplane

The first ad in the
inflight magazine reads
Beaver Creek beckons.
Yes. I've felt Its calling
for years.

What I Learned in Vermont

I welcome the stranger to
the seat next to me with a friendly
welcome to the row.

He says *right,* as if
I was just kidding. Apparently, he
is not from Vermont where

after a *welcome to the row* there
would have been a hug and maybe
a tongue kiss.

Crap

I think I forgot to mention
anything about *Professor Clown*.
Oh well. Ask me about it
when you see me.

(Upon checking further I realized I had mentioned
Professor Clown on page 79. But by then it was too
late to remove this poem.)

The author standing in front of Norman Rockwell's studio front door.

About The Author

Two-time Pushcart Prize nominee Rick Lupert has been involved in the Los Angeles poetry community since 1990. He was awarded the Beyond Baroque Distinguished Service Award in 2014 for service to the Los Angeles poetry community. He served for two years as a co-director of the non-profit literary organization Valley Contemporary Poets. His poetry has appeared in numerous magazines and literary journals, including *The Los Angeles Times, Rattle, Chiron Review, Red Fez, Zuzu's Petals, Stirring, The Bicycle Review, Caffeine Magazine, Blue Satellite* and others. He edited the anthologies *Ekphrastia Gone Wild - Poems Inspired by Art, A Poet's Haggadah: Passover through the Eyes of Poets*, and *The Night Goes on All Night - Noir Inspired Poetry*, and is the author of nineteen other books: *Donut Famine, Romancing the Blarney Stone, Making Love to the 50 Ft. Woman, The Gettysburg Undress* (Rothco Press), *Nothing in New England is New, Death of a Mauve Bat, Sinzibuckwud!, We Put Things In Our Mouths, Paris: It's The Cheese, I Am My Own Orange County, Mowing Fargo, I'm a Jew. Are You?, Feeding Holy Cats, Stolen Mummies, I'd Like to Bake Your Goods, A Man With No Teeth Serves Us Breakfast* (Ain't Got No Press), *Lizard King of the Laundromat, Brendan Constantine is My Kind of Town* (Inevitable Press) and *Up Liberty's Skirt* (Cassowary Press), and the spoken word album "Rick Lupert Live and Dead" (Ain't Got No Press). He hosted the long running Cobalt Café reading series in Canoga Park for almost twenty-one years and has read his poetry all over the world.

Rick created and maintains Poetry Super Highway, an online resource and publication for poets (PoetrySuperHighway.com), Haikuniverse, a daily online small poem publication (Haikuniverse.com), and writes and occasionally draws the daily web comic Cat and Banana with Brendan Constantine. (facebook.com/catandbanana) He also writes the weekly Jewish poetry blog "From the Lupertverse" for JewishJournal.com

Currently Rick works as a music teacher at synagogues in Southern California and as a graphic and web designer for anyone who would like to help pay his mortgage.

Rick's Other Books and Recordings

Donut Famine
Rothco Press ~ December, 2016

Romancing the Blarney Stone
Rothco Press ~ December, 2016

Rick Lupert Live and Dead (Album)
Ain't Got No Press ~ March, 2016

Making Love to the 50 Ft. Woman
Rothco Press ~ May, 2015

The Gettysburg Undress
Rothco Press ~ May, 2014

Ekphrastia Gone Wild (edited by)
Ain't Got No Press ~ July, 2013

Nothing in New England is New
Ain't Got No Press ~ March, 2013

Death of a Mauve Bat
Ain't Got No Press ~ January, 2012

**The Night Goes On All Night
Noir Inspired Poetry** (edited by)
Ain't Got No Press ~ November, 2011

Sinzibuckwud!
Ain't Got No Press ~ January, 2011

We Put Things In Our Mouths
Ain't Got No Press ~ January, 2010

A Poet's Haggadah (edited by)
Ain't Got No Press ~ April, 2008

**A Man With No Teeth
Serves Us Breakfast**
Ain't Got No Press ~ May, 2007

I'd Like to Bake Your Goods
Ain't Got No Press ~ January, 2006

Stolen Mummies
Ain't Got No Press ~ February, 2003

Brendan Constantine is My Kind of Town
Inevitable Press ~ September, 2001

Up Liberty's Skirt
Cassowary Press ~ March, 2001

Feeding Holy Cats
Cassowary Press ~ May, 2000

I'm a Jew, Are You?
Cassowary Press ~ May, 2000

Mowing Fargo
Sacred Beverage Press ~ December, 1998

Lizard King of the Laundromat
The Inevitable Press ~ February, 1998

I Am My Own Orange County
Ain't Got No Press ~ May, 1997

Paris: It's The Cheese
Ain't Got No Press ~ May, 1996

For more information:
http://PoetrySuperHighway.com/

www.ingramcontent.com/pod-product-compliance
Lightning Source LLC
Chambersburg PA
CBHW071726080526
44588CB00013B/1914